AF488114

Two Kids on a Whiteboard: Do This Try That

By

Mike J. Preble

Copyright
©2022 Mike J. Preble
All rights reserved
Engaging the Underachiever, LLC
Bloomington, Minnesota
USA
Toss
Golf
&
Croquet

Two Kids on a Whiteboard
Do This. Try That.

Dedicated to:

Learners, and those willing to help learners learn.

Water

Water goes downhill, always. A flowing
river is going downhill.

Measure and pour water.

Make a river.

Make boats that float.

Plants and Flowers

The best way to learn flower names is to learn
one. Dandelion. That's an easy one to remember.
Then another, like Daisy. Now you know two.
Add a third: Sun Flower. And a fourth: Tulips.
This next one's a bit hard: Hydrangea.
Oh, look. A Day Lily.

Ball Games

A bounce pass is easier to throw and catch.
Use two hands to throw and two hands to catch.

Kites and Air Planes

Let the string out, slowly.
The wind will take it.
There you go. Nice job.
Hold tight, but don't hurt your fingers.

12
9
3
6
100
10

Making Games

It's called "Drop the Clothespin".

You have to reach over the chair and "Drop the Clothespin" into the jar.

Playground

Are you nervous? Don't be afraid. I will catch you.

I'll count to three, and when I say 'three', you let go.

Ready?

One.

Two…,

Go Back 3
!
Lose Turn
5
2
4

Spinner Games

That was fun.

I almost won, but then I got "Go Back 3" and landed in Quick Sand.

And then you spun an 8.

I'm hungry. How about a snack?

Bowling

Take aim and roll the ball.
Not too fast.
There you go.
Oooooh!

Weaving

It's called "Paper Plate Weaving". The string goes over-under, over-under.

This is good practice for learning how to tie your shoe.

Speaking of which…,

ENTRANCE
← →

Mobiles (and Balance)

Wow. A giant mobile.
Everything's swimming round and round.
There's the entrance.

You know what? When we get back home, we should make a mobile. All you need is a stick, some string and some things (and balance).

root | flower | leaf | stem
Cut & Paste &
What is the next shape?
Moon Star circle square

Cut and Paste

    I bought you a "Cut and Paste" book. You cut
things out and paste them where they belong.
    I'll help you get started, if you like.
    This first one's about shape patterns.

Apples (Pies and Wagons)

I'll hold you up. You pick. Get the reddest apples you can reach.

We'll take a few from the ground and then be on our way.

We're going to "Apple Pie City".

I'll even show you how to use the apple peeler.